McCurdy and the Silver Dart

McCURDY

AND

THE SILVER DART

Les Harding

UNIVERSITY COLLEGE OF CAPE BRETON PRESS

The UCCB Press acknowledges the support received for its publishing program
from the Canada Council's Block Grants program.

Cover illustration by Patsy MacAulay MacKinnon
Cover design by Ryan Astle, Goose Lane Editions
Book designed by Carl Getto
Printed and bound in Canada by University of Toronto Press

Canadian Cataloguing in Publication Data

Harding, Les, 1950-

McCurdy and the Silver Dart

Includes bibliographical references.
ISBN 0-920336-69-8

1. McCurdy, J. A. D. (John Alexander Douglas), 1886-1961 - - Juvenile
literature. 2. Silver Dart (Airplane) - - Juvenile literature. 3. Aeronautics - -
Canada - - History - - Juvenile literature. I. Title.

TL540 . M23H37 1998   j629 . 13 ' 092   C98-950232-5

University College of Cape Breton Press
Box 5300
Sydney, Nova Scotia, Canada
B 1P 6L2

Acknowledgements

Chapter heading plane drawings from National Aviation
Museum Web Site.
http://www.nmstc.ca/nam/educ/history/3silv.html

Alexander Graham Bell National Historic Site, Baddeck, N.S.

Public Archives of Nova Scotia, Halifax, N.S.

TABLE OF CONTENTS

Chapter 1
Helping the Great Inventor........................... *9*

Chapter 2
Kites and Gliders..................................... *25*

Chapter 3
Success and Danger................................. *43*

Chapter 4
The Silver Dart....................................... *55*

Chapter 5
The Army Says 'No' *65*

Chapter 6
Barnstorming.. *75*

Chapter 7
Triumph and Treachery In Cuba.................*89*

Chapter 8
McCurdy and World War 1.......................*103*

Chapter 9
Silver Dart Flies Again............................ *111*

Endnotes.. *119*
Bibliography...*121*
Glossary...*123*

Chapter 1

Helping the Great

Inventor

John Alexander Douglas McCurdy was born on August 2, 1886, in the hamlet of Baddeck, Cape Breton Island. His father, Arthur, was a part-time inventor who held a valuable patent for developing photographic film. His grandfather had been a distinguished member of the Nova Scotia Assembly for over forty years. An aunt, Georgina McCurdy, was one of the founders of the Victorian Order of Nurses.

Because Douglas came from a family of high achievers everyone in Baddeck sensed he was destined for greatness—but in what field? Perhaps he would be a scientist or an inventor like his father. As a child Douglas, as he was called, was filled with an insatiable curiosity to know how things worked. But he was also stubborn and mischievous.

Though no one realised it yet, Douglas' course in life had already been set. A year before his birth, in the summer of 1885, a chance and seemingly unimportant meeting occurred which was to have a profound effect on the future of Douglas McCurdy.

The editor of the local newspaper, *The Cape Breton Island Reporter*, was angrily shaking a newfangled gizmo lately installed in his office. The gizmo, the first in that part of Cape Breton Island, was called a telephone. It was not working, although it had been in fine working order earlier that morning. What could have gone wrong?

The editor, preoccupied as he was, did not notice the approach of a tall, well-dressed, bewhiskered stranger who was peering at him through the window with evident interest. Without waiting to be asked, the stranger entered the office.

"Having trouble with your telephone?" the stranger asked in a soft Scottish accent.

The editor, startled at the approach of the stranger, replied that indeed he was having trouble and feared that he would have to travel all the way to Halifax to get the instrument repaired.

"Let me have a look at it," said the stranger,

with a hint of a smile on his face. The stranger glanced at the receiver for barely a moment. Expertly, he unscrewed the mouthpiece, flicked a dead fly out and reassembled it.

"It'll work now," he said.

The editor placed a call. Sure enough, the telephone was as good as new.

The dumbfounded editor could not resist asking the question, "How do you know so much about the telephone?"

"I invented it." [1]

The newspaper editor was Douglas McCurdy's father and the stranger was Alexander Graham Bell, the man who had invented the telephone only nine years before.

Bell was in Cape Breton Island looking for a

place to build a summer home. At the age of thirty-eight he was already a wealthy man and one of the most famous inventors in history. Bell eventually chose to settle in Baddeck because of its resemblance to Scotland, the land of his birth. Near the village Bell purchased a tract of land from McCurdy's grandfather on which he constructed a fine home called Beinn Bhreagh, which in the Gaelic language of Scotland means "beautiful mountain."

It was here that Bell built a laboratory to carry on his scientific experiments into the possibility of manned flight. Douglas' life would be changed because of Bell's settling in Baddeck. He and Bell became great friends. Growing up at Bell's side helped Douglas choose what work he would do when he became older.

Kite flying was a popular activity during those days when Bell and Douglas became actively interested in developing a plane. By flying kites Douglas learned about wind and air currents. The picture above shows a tetrahedron kite flying near Baddeck around 1907. (Photo courtesy Alexander Graham Bell National Historic Site, Baddeck, N.S.)

Bell was determined to crown his career as an inventor with the construction of a heavier-than-air flying machine. He was one of many researchers trying to discover the secrets of wind currents and air pressure. As a small boy Douglas took an active role helping the great Dr. Bell on experiments with different shaped flying kites. How many scientists and professors the world over would have gladly traded places with the boy from Baddeck?

Douglas also participated in some of the earliest attempts ever made to record the human voice on wax discs. McCurdy took an impish delight in watching Dr. Bell astonish the local farmers by playing back to them the Gaelic songs they had been coaxed into singing moments before.

Because of the presence of Bell, important

visitors were drawn to Baddeck. Among these were Lord Aberdeen, the Governor General, and Sir Wilfrid Laurier, the Prime Minister of Canada. People came from all over Cape Breton Island to welcome such distinguished visitors. Somehow, amidst the thronging crowds of adults, Douglas succeeded in getting close enough to Prime Minister Laurier to shake his hand. The boy was so thrilled at the honour that he was reluctant to wash his hand for some time after.

On another occasion, Douglas, while visiting Beinn Bhreagh, was introduced to two famous scientists: Professor Samuel Langley, secretary of the Smithsonian Institute in Washington and Simon Newcomb, born in Nova Scotia, and professor at Johns Hopkins University in Baltimore, Maryland. Two more opposing personalities could not be imagined. It was interesting that they were visiting Dr. Bell at the same time. Langley shared Bell's belief, and shared it passionately, that someday it would be possible for people to fly in heavier-than-air flying machines. He had already conducted a number of important experiments to prove his point. Newcomb, on the other hand, was just as convinced that human flight in general, and Langley's theories in particular were quite impossible. They simply violated the laws of physics.

Voices were soon raised and Dr. Bell became alarmed that his guests were conducting their aeronautical arguments a little too hotly. Bell wanted to find another, safer, topic of conversation so he started talking about cats. Langley remarked how strange it was that cats always landed on their feet when dropped from a height. Newcomb immediately adopted the opposite position. "Nonsense," he cried, "where's the fulcrum? How can a falling cat turn itself without a fulcrum?" [2] A fulcrum is a support, which allows an object to turn around.

Bell figured that the only way to make peace between his scientific houseguests was to put the argument to the test and prove or disprove it scientifically. Bell had Douglas and his housekeeper collect about a dozen squirming cats and place them in a basket. Bell was a great cat lover. His estate was filled with cats.

But the cats would not stay in the basket. It must have been a funny sight to see three scientists chasing cats around a room. Finally, the scientists succeeded in herding the cats onto a balcony which was about six metres from the ground. Douglas helped the housekeeper spread some of Mrs. Bell's best cushions below the balcony. The experiment proved that Langley was correct. All the cats landed on their feet when dropped on to Mrs. Bell's soft cushions. Newcomb admitted that he had been wrong and thanked Langley for giving him an interesting new problem of physics to solve. It would be interesting to know what the young Douglas McCurdy thought while watching three famous scientists toss cats over a balcony.

Bell always had a fondness for children but sadly, his own two sons had died in infancy. Still, he especially liked Douglas and so when Douglas was five the Bells suggested they adopt him. Douglas' mother had died when he was two, while giving birth to his brother Lucian. With Arthur McCurdy employed as Bell's secretary and constant companion, it was felt that Douglas would never be far from his real father. But Aunt Georgina said "no." It was not right to split up a family. Douglas was born a McCurdy and must be raised as one.

In the fall of 1893, when the Bells returned to their winter home in Washington, D.C., it was agreed the McCurdy family would accompany them. One of the highlights of that year in Washington for Douglas was when Dr. Bell took him to the opening of the Volta Bureau, an institution, found by Bell, devoted to helping the deaf. (Mrs. Bell was deaf.) At the ceremony, Douglas met the famed blind and deaf girl Helen Keller and her teacher Annie Sullivan.

The next year, after the McCurdys returned to

Baddeck, Douglas had a very foolish idea. Imitating thescientists he had met, Douglas decided to play inventor by making fireworks to celebrate a playmate's birthday. After first picking the lock to his father's hunting room, Douglas collected ammunition and then gunpowder. He then tossed a lighted match onto the powder. The bang was tremendous. The force of the explosion shattered windows all over Baddeck. When the smoke cleared Douglas was unconscious and near death. The boy's eyebrows had been singed off by the blast and the entire right side of his body had been burned black. There was a danger that he might lose an eye. Happily, after a few days in a darkened room, with his eyes wrapped in bandages, his sight returned and he regained full consciousness. His right hand however, had taken the full force of the explosion and was horribly mangled. Signs of gangrene, a serious tissue killing disease caused by infection or the impairment of blood circulation, set in and the three doctors in attendance decided to amputate at the wrist.

The operation was to take place the next morning at eleven and the shocking news spread over the community of Baddeck like a shroud. When Graham Bell heard of it he raced to the young patient's bedside and grilled the doctors as to Douglas' condition. Learning that the injured hand had not grown any worse during the previous 24 hours he asked the doctors if the boy's life would be in danger if the operation was held off for another day. The doctors concluded that Douglas' life was not in immediate danger so, somewhat reluctantly, they agreed to Bell's request and delayed the amputation.

The extra day passed and Douglas' hand did not grow any worse. It was then decided to postpone the operation indefinitely. Instead a medication of lard and boric acid was applied regularly to the wound. The recovery was long and painful but after six months, Douglas was completely healthy. Thanks to the timely interference of Alexander Graham Bell his hand was strong and whole.

Throughout the rest of his life, Douglas never forgot the lesson he learned. While he kept his love of adventure and spirit of curiosity, he now had a healthy dose of caution and common sense to go with it.

Chapter 2

Kites and Gliders

In 1903, at the age of 16, Douglas left Baddeck to attend the University of Toronto's School of Mechanical Engineering. Of all the students admitted to the University that year, Douglas was the youngest. Though he received excellent grades, Douglas did not like university. Instead he was more interested in summer vacations so he could work with the great Alexander Graham Bell.

In the summer of 1906 Douglas, knowing that Dr. Bell was always on the lookout for bright young engineering talent, invited a fellow student, Frederick Walker "Casey" Baldwin, to accompany him to Baddeck. Casey had never heard of Baddeck but he had heard of Alexander Graham Bell and jumped at the chance of meeting him. Casey, incidentally, was the grandson of Sir Robert Baldwin, pre-Confederation Prime Minister of Canada.

Upon their arrival in Cape Breton Island, the two young engineers began to work with Bell, studying the effect of air currents on tetrahedral structures. A tetrahedron is a triangle with four sides. The problem to be solved was one of weight and strength. A flying structure strong enough to carry a man was thought to be too heavy to fly. The

While studying wind currents Bell, Douglas, and their associates developed kites of many different sizes and styles. The kite shown in this photo is certainly one of their more unusual shapes. (Photo courtesy Alexander Graham Bell National Historic Site, Baddeck, N.S.)

solution to this problem was the tetrahedron. Douglas' experiments showed that a skeleton frame of tetrahedrons, with each side equal in size, connected together at the corners, was both strong enough and light enough to do the job. It also possessed a remarkable degree of stability and so was ideal for a powered flying machine.

Because Douglas, Casey, and Bell did not have much experience with engines, they invited Glenn Curtiss, a manufacturer of motorcycle engines from Hammondsport, New York, to join the group in the spring of 1907. Curtiss was an expert on light and compact engines.

Another expert—this one from the United States Army—would soon be asked to join the group. While the Government of Canada was sceptical about manned flight, the United States government's position was encouraging. There the War Department had already conducted flying experiments. The Aeronautical Division of the United States Army had just been started for the purpose of developing balloons and flying machines for military use. Lieutenant Thomas Selfridge was a graduate of the West Point military academy and a member of the Fifth Field Artillery. As an expert in the science of aerodynamics, he was sent to observe the kite experiments in Baddeck. As Selfridge's knowledge of kite flying was second only to his own, Bell invited him to work in Baddeck and join Douglas and Casey. Such was Alexander Graham Bell's stature that, upon receiving a request from him, the President of the United States, Theodore Roosevelt, immediately placed Selfridge on indefinite leave.

At the same time, Mrs. Bell suggested an association be formed. To finance the project Mrs. Bell sold a piece of property she had inherited for $25,000 and then donated an additional $10,000. So on October 1, 1907, the Aerial Experiment Association was born. The A.E.A. was incorporated in both Canada and the United States, as a "co-operative scientific association, not for gain but for the love of the art and doing what we can to help one another." [1] The five members were to be called associates. Dr. Bell was chairman and Douglas the treasurer. Glenn Curtiss was to receive $5,000 for taking time away from his factory in Hammondsport. Douglas and Baldwin would each receive $1,000, while Lieutenant Selfridge would continue to draw

The Aerial Experiment Association was formed in 1907 with the goal of "getting a man into the air." Members of the Association are shown above. From left to right: Glenn Curtiss, F.W. "Casey" Baldwin, Alexander Graham Bell, Thomas Selfridge, and J.A.D. McCurdy. (Photo courtesy Alexander Graham Bell National Historic Site, Baddeck, N.S.)

his pay from the United States Army. The aim of the Aerial Experiment Association was simple: "getting a man into the air." [2]

The associates set to work testing engines and propellers. They also towed model kites from speedboats to measure the effects of wind velocities and air currents. These experiments led to the building of a giant man-carrying tetrahedral kite *Cygnet 1*, also known as " the little swan." Douglas had helped Bell fly kites on the hills around Baddeck for years but never anything like the *Cygnet 1*. The "little swan" was an enormous and ungainly contraption with a wingspan of 13 metres. Looking like a honeycomb sliced open, the *Cygnet 1* was made up of 3,000 tetrahedral cells covered in bright red silk.

Yet for all the painstaking effort that went into

The tetrahedral kite the Cygnet 1 is shown while participating in an experiment to study wind current. The photo was taken on August 9, 1907. There was no pilot in the kite at this time but there would be three months later. (Photo courtesy Alexander Graham Bell National Historic Site, Baddeck, N.S.)

the building of the *Cygnet 1*, little thought was given to the comfort of the pilot. There was no cockpit offering protection from the elements only open space just big enough for the pilot to crawl into and lie face down.

December 6, 1907, was the day fixed for the *Cygnet 1's* test flight. Douglas and the other associates decided that Thomas Selfridge, because of his familiarity with kites, should be the pilot. The weather was so frigid that Thomas had to wrap himself up in rugs to keep warm. The *Cygnet 1* was placed aboard a flat-bottomed boat called the *Ugly Duckling*, which was towed behind the steamboat *Blue Hill*. A sturdy rope connected the kite to the steamboat. In case of emergency, the rope connection with the steamboat would be the only

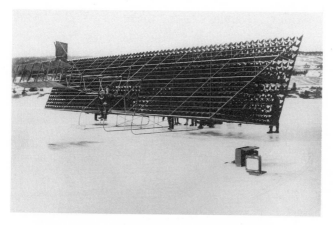

The Cygnet 1 is shown above preparing one of its flights over frozen Baddeck Bay in February, 1909. Douglas is the pilot in this picture. (Photo courtesy Alexander Graham Bell National Historic Site, Baddeck, N.S.)

way of controlling the kite.

Bell posed the important question: what would happen to a person if an accident occurred when he was being propelled through the air with the speed of a locomotive? Because he was also concerned about an accident, Douglas wanted these early flights to take place over water.

The pilot had little control. Selfridge, lodged in the centre of hundreds of flapping red silk cells could see virtually nothing. If the kite was tipped to one side by an unexpected wind, all the pilot could do was shift his body weight in the hope of straightening the *Cygnet 1*. The pilot had no other means of control. Selfridge was especially brave, knowing he was more of a passenger than a pilot.

The *Blue Hill* steamed through the choppy waters of the Bras d'Or Lakes pulling the boat which carried the *Cygnet 1*. Everyone waited for a good wind. Then without warning the *Cygnet 1* caught a gust and soared into the air. Douglas was jubilant because thanks to his efforts a member

The Blue Hill (the white steamer) is shown pulling the boat the Ugly Duckling on which rests the Cygnet 1 whose pilot was waiting for a gust of wind to take the kite into the air. The Cygnet 1 was made of 3,000 tetrahedral cells. This photo was taken December 6, 1907. (Photo courtesy Alexander Graham Bell National Historic Site, Baddeck, N.S.)

of the Aerial Experiment Association was airborne. In less than a minute Thomas climbed to the dizzying height of 51 metres and attained a speed of 19 kilometres per hour. The kite sailed smoothly for about seven minutes. Suddenly, the *Cygnet 1* pitched on its nose and hurtled downward out of control. As the kite neared the surface of the water a cloud of black smoke from the steamer's funnel blocked everyone's view. The crewman on the *Blue Hill*, who had been assigned the duty of cutting the tow line with an axe in case of trouble, could also not see the kite and so he did not cut the rope. No one was aware that the *Cygnet 1* had crashed and was being dragged and bounced along the surface of the lake.

When the kite was reached, it was clear Thomas was lucky to have survived. The only thing that saved him was that he had kicked off his heavy oilskin boots moments before the flight. It was bad enough to be dunked into the ice cold waters of the Bras d'Or Lakes in December without being weighted down by water filled boots.

The kite was wrecked but the experiment was a success: it proved a person could glide through the sky. As a result of the accident, the group felt further work with kites and gliders were needed before an engine could be placed on one.

As part of their next step, Douglas and the other associates decided to spend the winter in Hammondsport, New York, near Curtiss' engine factory. Hammondsport was built on a lake and surrounded by snow covered hills that would be perfect for gliding. The availability of snow was a very important consideration. A soft place to land—or crash—was a definite advantage.

During the first months of 1908, Douglas, Bell, Thomas, Casey and Curtiss constructed a small double winged glider, which came to be known as the *Hammondsport Glider*. Constructed out of bamboo slats and nainsook, a soft cotton cloth, the *Hammondsport Glider* was as primitive an affair as one could imagine. Essentially, it was a pair of biplane wings fitted over the shoulders of the pilot, which left his legs free. The means of getting airborne was simple. With a man holding each wing tip for support, Douglas would fit himself into the wings, take a running leap off a hillside and hope for the best. Crack-ups were many but the deep banks of snow prevented any major injuries.

The biggest problem proved to be the craft's instability. When a tail was added control of the glider was improved dramatically. Over 50 flights were made, many of them covering as many as 35 metres, including one by Douglas of 91 metres.

Bell, a stickler for detail, insisted that careful notes be kept on everything that happened. The results of the experiments were recorded in the Aerial Experiment Association's weekly bulletin. Gradually, the group compiled the knowledge needed to improve their flight experiments.

And although the *Hammondsport Glider* was destroyed in an accident in the spring of 1909, the associates now had considerable knowledge. They felt they were now ready for powered flight.

Chapter 3

Success and Danger

The Aerial Experiment Association was set up so each of the associates could design his own airplane. But actually everyone helped each other. Douglas worked on all the projects, as did each of the other associates.

The associates' first aircraft was Thomas Selfridge's *Red Wing*. The name was derived from the red silk used to cover the wings. It was the same red silk left over from the *Cygnet 1*. The *Red Wing* was a biplane with a 13 metre wingspan, tail, rudder, tubular iron runners to help in landing, and a kitchen chair with the legs cut off as a cockpit for the pilot. The craft had a propeller of galvanised sheet metal and was powered by a small air-cooled eight-cylinder motorcycle engine of only 20 horsepower.

The date set for the *Red Wing's* first flight was March 12, 1908. There was so much excitement in the air that perhaps even the *Red Wing* itself was affected. As soon as the engine was started the *Red Wing* shot off down the ice of frozen Lake Keuka before anyone had time to climb into the cockpit! It even rose a metre or so into the air before settling down.

Fortunately, Douglas was wearing his skates. He raced after the runaway airplane, grabbed it by the tail and brought it back to the starting point.

The Wright Brothers, Wilbur and Orville, had been flying for several years in Kitty Hawk, North Carolina, but always in private. By way of contrast, there were several hundred spectators on hand to see the *Red Wing's* flight. It was the first public demonstration of flight in North America.

As Thomas was away at the time, someone else was needed to be the pilot. Douglas was keen for the honour himself but the choice fell on his friend Casey. The reason for Casey's selection had nothing to do with his piloting skill. Casey had forgotten his skates and could barely stand up on the ice. The cockpit of the *Red Wing* was the only "safe" place for him.

Casey climbed into the pilot's seat and

shouted, "Let's go!" This time several men held the wings, to hold the machine back, while the engine was reved up. At a signal, Douglas and his helpers released their grip and the *Red Wing* bounded forward. It roared along the ice for 45 metres and then rose smoothly into the air. Casey Baldwin had become the first Canadian to fly an airplane. He flew for about 100 metres, at an altitude of about three metres. Fortunately, there was no wind and so when the engine cut out Casey was able to glide to a safe landing.

Five days later on St. Patrick's Day, Casey was again at the controls of the *Red Wing* but this time he was not so lucky. As he came in for a landing a stiff breeze flipped the aircraft on its side. The *Red Wing* struck the ice with its wing and was destroyed.

*The pictures above show the Red Wing on March 17, 1908
before take off, crashing, and the remaining wreckage. Casey
Baldwin, the pilot, survived the crash. (Photo courtesy
Alexander Graham Bell National Historic Site, Baddeck, N.S.)*

Miraculously, Casey escaped the accident unhurt. It was obvious to Douglas and the shaken Casey that some form of lateral control was needed. Shifting the pilot's weight to compensate for the wind was not good enough.

The next machine in the air was Casey's own *White Wing*. Covered with white silk, as the supply of red had been used up, the *White Wing* resembled the *Red Wing* but with several technical advancements. The machine was equipped with a throttle and a triangular undercarriage supported by pneumatic bicycle tires. But the most important innovation was the moveable wing tips called "little wings" or ailerons.

The aileron was undoubtedly Douglas and his associates' greatest contribution to the story of flight.

The principle was extremely simple. Straps were connected from the wing tips to the pilot's shoulders by means of a yoke. If one wing began to dip in the wind, the pilot simply leaned in the opposite direction. The pull on the ailerons would stabilise the aircraft and compensate for the dip.

There is an interesting story of how the aileron came to be named. Henri Farman, a French aviator, was in New York City demonstrating an aircraft he had been racing in Europe. He made a flight down the length of a field, landed, had his airplane turned around by hand, took off again and flew back to his starting point. Douglas was curious as to why Farman had landed halfway through the flight. Why had he simply not turned around in the air? The Frenchman was alarmed at the suggestion. "No, no! It was impossible," he said. "The aircraft would tip over." Douglas, who did not speak much French, had difficulty explaining to Farman his work on moveable wing tips. At last, Douglas said, "little wings." "Ah, ailerons," said Farman, translating Douglas' words. Newspaper reporters, witnessing the discussion, spread the story and the new word. [1]

It took two months to build the *White Wing*. Casey first flew it, on May 18, 1908. Douglas at 24 years old was the youngest of the associates and had not yet flown an engine powered machine. He made his first powered flight on May 23—it was nearly his last. Apart from almost killing himself, he wrecked the *White Wing* beyond repair and came close to killing Thomas. It was not a very promising beginning for the man destined to become the greatest flyer of his time.

What happened was that with Douglas in the cockpit for the first time in his life, Thomas and his dog walked in front of the aircraft to determine the precise spot it would leave the ground. The engine was started and Douglas zoomed down the field. In his excitement Douglas did not see Thomas and aimed the rolling plane at him. Thomas dived to the ground as the *White Wing* roared over him with only centimetres to spare. Douglas vaguely remembered seeing a dog.

The flight was a success but the landing a disaster. Here is Douglas' description of the accident:

> It was a comparatively calm day, the wind only coming in puffs, but it was through one of these puffs that the machine met its Waterloo. Curtiss started the engine and, as in previous

trials, a half dozen men held the plane till the engine was developing its full power. She then ran along the ground and left it so smoothly that I didn't realise we were in the air.

The machine took a slight turn to the left and then curved round to the right. The wind blew about on the left quarter, and as she turned to the right, another puff elevated the left wing, depressing the right so much that it caught in the grass. I leaned to the high side with the idea of adjusting the tips so that a righting could be produced, but as I was sitting too far forward, my back failed to engage the lever, which operates the tips, and so no righting result was produced.

As the right wing struck the ground, the machine pivoted and the nose swung around and dug into the ground. I was deposited gently and without much of a jar on the ground.

The machine turned a complete somersault almost over me, but left me free of the debris. [2]

The third A.E.A. aircraft was Curtiss' *June Bug*. This was the most successful. It was built solidly and never crashed, although flown over 100 times. Douglas made up for his calamitous beginning by becoming the most accomplished flyer of the group. He flew the *June Bug* on flights of up to three kilometres, an incredible distance for those days. On one flight he executed the very first figure eight.

During the summer of 1908, Douglas changed the *June Bug's* name to *Loon*. He fitted the aircraft with two light pontoons, intending to convert it into a seaplane. It was an interesting attempt but proved unsuccessful. The aircraft was so underpowered that Douglas was unable to get the *Loon* into the air.

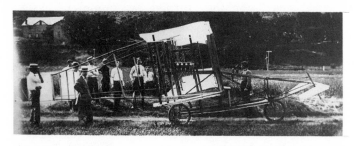

The June Bug had great success in 1908 at the A.E.A.'s base in New York state. The plane was flown more than 100 times without crashing. It also flew three kilometers with McCurdy as pilot. (Photo courtesy Alexander Graham Bell National Historic Site, Baddeck, N.S.)

But while had group was having success, tragedy was about to strike. On a visit to Washington, Thomas accepted an invitation to be a passenger in an airplane flown by Orville Wright. At a height of 25 metres the engine stalled; the aircraft nosed into a dive and crashed. Orville Wright was seriously injured; Thomas was killed. Thomas Selfridge became the first person to be killed in the crash of an airplane.

Chapter 4

The Silver Dart

The surviving members of the Aerial Experiment Association deeply felt the loss of Thomas but the work had to continue—Thomas would have wanted it that way.

Now it was Douglas' turn to design an airplane. He called his plane the *Silver Dart*. The Silver in the name came from a coloured rubber compound applied to the wings and the Dart because it seemed appropriate. The *Silver Dart* had a wingspan of 13 metres, weighed 436 kilograms and was powered by a 35 horsepower water-cooled engine, the first of its kind in the world. While piloting the *June Bug,* Douglas had the frightening experience of having his engine fail in mid-air because of an excessive build up of heat. The water-cooled engine would hopefully prevent this from happening again.

The *Silver Dart* made its first flight in Hammondsport on December 6, 1908. Over the next few weeks, Douglas flew his plane nine times, once for a distance of two kilometres. But by now he was growing homesick for Nova Scotia, so he crated the *Silver Dart* and shipped it to Baddeck. When the *Silver Dart* reached the border the Canadian customs officials scratched their heads in disbelief. They did not know what to make of this strange contraption. In vain, they leafed through their rulebooks trying to find a category to place it under. Eventually they decided that the *Silver Dart* must be a luxury good and Douglas would have to pay a heavy duty. Douglas argued otherwise. With some misgivings, the customs officials relented. The *Silver Dart* was allowed to enter Canada duty-free but only because Douglas promised to take it out of the country in less than a year's time.

On February 23, 1909, Douglas was ready to take the *Silver Dart* for its first flight at Baddeck. A local man, John MacDermid, used his horse and sleigh to tow the *Silver Dart* to a spot on the ice of the Bras d'Or Lake near a place called Fraser's Pond.

It was a brisk and sunny winter's day. There

Douglas McCurdy is shown at the controls of the Silver Dart in 1908. In this plane McCurdy became the ninth person ever to fly and the first person to fly in Canada. (Photo courtesy Alexander Graham Bell National Historic Site, Baddeck, N.S.)

was excitement in the crowd of onlookers, as well as a good deal of scoffing disbelief. The area schools were adjourned for the day and the entire town of Baddeck was closed down to witness the event, if event it was to be. Though the flight was not scheduled until the afternoon, the crowd, many of who were on skates or in sleighs, had been gathering on the lake since morning. Nervously, Douglas was making last minute adjustments to his machine and looking at the weather. Most of all he was waiting for the arrival of Alexander Graham Bell. At three o'clock Dr. Bell, nearly buried in a massive fur coat, arrived by horse and sleigh. McCurdy climbed into the cockpit and was ready to go. Bell, ever cautious, suggested that he wait for a medical doctor to arrive—just in case. Dr. Dan MacDonald arrived a few minutes later. Douglas, wearing a stocking cap over his ears, gave the signal and waved the crowd off. Someone spun the propeller and the engine sputtered and coughed into life. A cloud of smoke and snow covered many of the onlookers who had not moved far enough away. Eight helpers held the aircraft in place while it built up sufficient power. At Douglas' signal they let go and the *Silver Dart* raced across the ice—for 30 metres.

Much to the delight of some members of the watching crowd, the *Silver Dart* had ground to a halt with a broken gasoline pump. Douglas, ignoring a few wisecracks, quickly repaired the damage and had the *Silver Dart* wheeled around and towed back to its starting position.

The *Silver Dart* was pointed into the wind for a second time. The propeller was cranked and the little engine revved up. When the helpers let go of their grip the *Silver Dart* leaped forward for about 50 metres and then...sailed smoothly into the air.

The crowd went wild. A mob of men and boys

Above: *The Silver Dart prepares to take off from the frozen Bras d'Or Lakes in Baddeck on February, 1909.*
Below: *The Silver Dart is airborne with Douglas McCurdy at the controls. This was the first airplane flight ever in Canada. (Photo courtesy Alexander Graham Bell National Historic Site, Baddeck, N.S.)*

on their skates chased after Douglas, disbelieving their eyes. They did not understand it but there he was a local boy from Baddeck flying through the air!

Douglas flew for about one kilometre, at a height of 20 metres and a speed of 65 kilometres per hour. The people of Baddeck, indeed the people of Canada, had never seen anything like it before. John Alexander Douglas McCurdy had just made the first flight in Canada and the first anywhere in the British Empire. He was only the ninth person in the world to fly an airplane.

After scarcely more than a minute in the air, Douglas made a perfect three point landing and taxied to his starting point. The flight happened so quickly and unexpectedly that he had almost clipped one doubter who had started for home in his horse and sleigh.

The onlookers had been converted into believers and they wanted more. Douglas was ready to give it to them until Dr. Bell stood up in his sleigh and said that it would be best to call it a day. There was no reason to tempt fate. History had been made in Baddeck and that was enough for one day. McCurdy promised everyone that the *Silver Dart* would fly again tomorrow.

Bell invited everyone back to his laboratory, where he made a suitable speech to mark the occasion. Douglas was the hero of the hour. All those present were asked to sign a book that would commemorate the event and honour the daring young aviator. The formalities over, the guests were served tea and coffee, sandwiches and homemade raspberry vinegar, a drink to which the teetotaling Dr. Bell was very partial. Of the 147 people who signed the book of commemoration, no less than 74 names began with the syllable Mc and of those 16 were McDonald.

The next day Douglas kept his promise and took the *Silver Dart* for a flight of six kilometres. On the third day he astonished everyone by flying 30 kilometres non-stop!

Newspapers from around the world heralded the young Canadian aviator from Baddeck.

Chapter 5

The Army Says "No"

In March 31, 1909, the Aerial Experiment Association, having more than fulfilled its mission to get a man into the air was allowed to expire. The same day Douglas and Casey, with assistance from Dr. Bell, formed the Canadian Aerodrome Company for the purpose of manufacturing airplanes in Canada.

Douglas was determined to alert the Government of Canada to the airplane's exciting potential. To this end, he began a tour of the cities of eastern Canada. In each city, he used the *Silver Dart* to put on a demonstration flight.

Meanwhile, Alexander Graham Bell did what he could to help on the lecture circuit. On March 27, 1909, he spoke before the Canadian Club of Ottawa. Listening to his address were Earl Grey, the Governor General; Prime Minister Laurier; Robert Borden, Leader of the Opposition; Sir Sandford Fleming, builder of the Canadian Pacific Railway; and a number of other dignitaries and government ministers. The Minister of Militia and Defence was also in attendance. Dr. Bell gave a ringing speech full of patriotism, praising the two young Canadian aviators,

McCurdy and Baldwin. He went on to stress the coming commercial and military importance of the airplane, concluding his talk with the stirring words, "The nation that controls the air will ultimately be the foremost nation of the world." [1]

From this speech came an invitation for Douglas and Casey to display their aircraft, at their own expense, for officials of the Ministry of Militia and Defence at the Petawawa military camp in northern Ontario.

Upon uncrating the *Silver Dart* in Petawawa, Douglas was pleased to see that a shed had been constructed for his use. It was the first aircraft hanger on Canadian soil. But everyone in Ottawa did not share the optimism felt by the two young pilots. There were many officials in both the government and the military who thought this business with airplanes to be a foolish waste of time and public money.

The date picked for the test flight was August 2, 1909. Douglas climbed into the cockpit of the *Silver Dart*, the propeller was spun, and he taxied off for the first of four successful flights. On hand to witness the event were about 40 newspaper reporters and photographers and the most senior military officers in the country.

Douglas flew along a course that was one kilometre long, at a speed of 70 kilometres per hour and at an altitude of 20 metres. The *Silver Dart* handled beautifully, displaying stability and manoeuvrability in the air. The observers on the ground had to admit that it was an impressive demonstration.

On the fifth flight of the day, Douglas' good fortune left him. As he came in for a landing, the sun momentarily blinded him. The wheels on the undercarriage ploughed into the soft sand covering the landing strip and the *Silver Dart* flipped over on its nose. The *Silver Dart* was destroyed in the accident and Douglas suffered a broken nose, the most serious injury of his flying career. After 300 flights, this was the *Silver Dart's* first and last mishap. A monument with a bronze plaque, in honour of the first military demonstration of aircraft flight in Canada, now marks the spot where the *Silver Dart* came to her end.

The military, for some unfathomable reason, decided that the fifth flight was the official flight. They ignored the earlier flights and decided that this was the only one from which they could make their assessment. They were not inclined to be generous with their comments. Much later, Douglas received a withering reply to his continuing efforts to attract the interest of the government of Canada. "The aeroplane is an invention of the devil and will never play any part in such a serious business as the defence of a nation, my boy!" [2]

Douglas's mishap with the *Silver Dart* was partially due to his unfamiliarity with the terrain and its unsuitability as a landing field. The field was sandy and uneven, normally used by the cavalry as a training ground.

Despite such serious setbacks, the Canadian Aerodrome Company of Baddeck, Nova Scotia, designed and built two aircraft, the *Baddeck 1* and the *Baddeck II*. Douglas decided to take another attempt at the government. The *Baddeck 1* had been shipped to Petawawa at the same time as the *Silver Dart*. The *Baddeck 1* was the first aircraft to be equipped with enclosed fuel tanks for greater safety. It was also the first to have elevators, or ailerons located at the rear of the plane. Douglas flew the *Baddeck 1* on August 11 and 12, 1909. Both flights were successful. On the flight of August 13, his engine stalled and the *Baddeck 1* crash landed after a flight of only 75 metres. Douglas was not injured but once again he had failed to impress the most senior military officers in Canada.

The *Baddeck 1* was repaired and in June, 1910, took part in the Montreal aviation meet, the first of its kind in Canada. After several days of good flying, Douglas was caught in a high wind and the

Baddeck 1 crashed. This time it was destroyed. Douglas, who endured no more crashes than any other aviator in those early days, nevertheless, lived a charmed life. He emerged from the wreckage unhurt.

Discouraged by his reception in Petawawa, he returned to Nova Scotia. *Baddeck II* was completed on September 11, 1909, then flown two weeks later. Over the next three months, Douglas and Casey made a great number of flights, all of them flawless, including one of 20 kilometres in November.

In Ottawa, there was at least one official who had been impressed. The Governor General, Earl Grey, had become so keen on flying that he journeyed to Baddeck by private rail car. In his honour, Douglas put on a special aerial display. The Governor General stayed for a week enjoying the McCurdy's hospitality.

During the early months of 1910, Douglas flew the *Baddeck II* 23 times without incident. He broke distance and speed records on almost every flight. The days of crash landings were not over yet but the airplane was becoming more reliable.

In March, 1910, Douglas received another important visitor, Major G. S. Maunsell, Director of Engineering Services for the Militia. Douglas took the Major airborne as a passenger on several flights. Major Maunsell returned to Ottawa enthusiastic about the future of the airplane. But the government would not be swayed, their answer was still no.

Douglas even offered to sell his aircraft to the government for the low price of $10,000. He further offered to train pilots to fly for free but was turned down on both offers.

The end was in sight for the Canadian Aerodrome Company. The company was forced to close its doors only a year after its birth. Douglas would have to try something else.

Chapter 6

Barnstorming

Disappointed by officialdom's response in Canada, Douglas decided to become a barnstormer: a form of aerial daredevil peculiar to the early days of flying. By 1910, flying had caught the imagination of the public. People would gather in thousands at parks, fairs and racetracks all over North America to see an airplane in flight and, if they were fortunate, get a ride in one. The admission fee for one of these events was usually a dollar. For a percentage of the receipts a barnstormer would take his fragile craft airborne and put on a display of hair-raising acrobatics—stalls, slow rolls, snap rolls, inverted flying—guaranteed to thrill and chill. For every swoop and dive the crowd would roar its approval and think its dollar well spent. As a barnstormer Douglas could earn a healthy income but there were dangers: 29 stunt flyers were killed in 1910, 83 in 1911 and 122 in 1912!

Douglas travelled to the United States, getting in touch with his old friend from the Aerial Experiment Association, Glenn Curtiss. As Douglas was probably the most skilled pilot in the world, Curtiss was glad to have him. Douglas became the star attraction of the Curtiss Exhibition Company. Paying crowds from as far afield as Quebec and Mexico City thronged to see Douglas and his airplane.

The physical arrangements for one of his performances were complicated. As he travelled with his own crew of skilled mechanics and helpers he had to be guaranteed $500 to pay his costs. At each stop his aircraft had to be uncrated, reassembled and then carefully tested. A suitable flying field had to be scouted out and a huge circus tent erected as headquarters. As always, there was the weather to worry about. At the conclusion of a performance, the tent had to be taken down, the aircraft gently taken apart, re-crated and shipped by train to the next city.

The business arrangements were not so complex. Upon arriving in a city, Douglas would approach a newspaper and arrange to have his visit sponsored as an advertising stunt. Douglas would get

Douglas McCurdy is shown at one of his barnstorming events where his plane races a car at Daytona Beach, Florida, in 1911. As shown, Douglas' barnstorming events attracted large crowds. (Photo courtesy Alexander Graham Bell National Historic Site, Baddeck, N.S.)

banner headlines—"Astonishing Birdman," "Death Mocker," "Acrobat of the Air"—crowds of people would flock to see his air show and the newspaper would get its publicity.

Douglas' favourite stunt, the one his audiences seemed to enjoy the most, was a little trick he called "battleship bombing." In the centre of a field he placed two canvasses about 25 metres apart. Each canvas was about three metres square and represented a battleship. The bombs he used were fresh fruit! Oranges were the preferred ammunition.

On the day of the show he would zoom low over the crowd. After making a few passes around the field, he would race toward the targets at about 60 kilometres per hour while suspending from his neck and resting on his lap a basket of fresh oranges. On his first sweep over the target he would grab hold of an orange and lob it at the imaginary smokestacks of his imaginary battleships. The oranges would splatter with great dramatic effect and Douglas, more often than not, would score a direct hit in the centre of one of the canvasses. On his second, third and succeeding passes, Douglas would continue to bomb his targets with oranges. The bombing would last until he had run out of fruit and his "battleship" had been "sunk" or, at least, covered in orange pulp. The crowds loved it.

Douglas was one of the few who realised it at the time, but political clouds were darkening. Only a few short years after these harmless displays of "battleship bombing" the savage slaughter of World War I erupted. Douglas' manoeuvres were destined to be repeated, but with deadly seriousness.

In August 1911, he was back in Canada attending a flying meet in Hamilton, Ontario. Despite some serious dangers, such as having his engine cut out at 100 metres and nearly having his plane burst into flames, the meet was a success.

The *Hamilton Herald* gives us a fairly typical description of one of Douglas' barnstorming performances:

He tore across the field at a terrific speed in his racing biplane and rose in the air at a speed of sixty miles [one hundred kilometres] an hour. He passed Willard when the latter was 400 feet [120 metres] in the air. After circling the field Willard decided to come down, after which McCurdy started out on a cross-country flight. He rose to a height of 2000 feet [600 metres] and went far out over the bay....When he descended he expressed entire satisfaction with the working of his machine. Willard was also astounded and said: "McCurdy's is the climbiest machine I ever saw. When he passed me at an altitude of 400 feet he was going at an awful speed and climbing straight up." [1]

The other pilot was Charles P. Willard, a well-known American aviator. The *Herald* continues its profile of Douglas:

> As a final wind-up, he decided to try a
> flight to see how high he could possibly
> go with his new machine. He started on
> his course far out over the lake, and
> circled back, soaring up to a height of
> 3000 feet [900 metres], but was forced
> to descend on account of the cold.
> When he landed his teeth were
> chattering and his hands were almost
> frozen. He said it was the first time he
> had ever been cold while in flight and
> that he was forced to descend on
> account of the frigid atmosphere,
> although his machine could have gone
> much higher. [2]

At the conclusion of the meet, Douglas and Willard, who were both scheduled to appear at a similar gathering in Toronto, decided to have a race. The course, Hamilton to Toronto, was the first aerial race in Canada and the longest cross-country flight up to that time.

Douglas had made Willard a small wager, betting his friend that he could give him a 10-minute head start and still beat him to Toronto. After Willard took off, a spectator in Hamilton called out to Douglas, "You'll never catch him now." Douglas replied, "I'll bet you a five spot I do." The onlooker accepted the bet and the race was on. [3]

Willard, flying at only 175 metres, took the cautious route following the rails of the Grand Trunk Railway. He encountered rainsqualls the whole way, having only five minutes of good flying.

Douglas, adventurous as usual, boldly cut across the end of Lake Ontario, cruising at 1000 metres. At that height, the air was clearer and he could see boats on the surface of the water quite distinctly. When he neared Toronto, Douglas hit a wave of warm air rising from the city. His machine began to vibrate uncontrollably. He concluded that the safe thing to do was to descend and take a lower stratum of air. This was fine except that the atmosphere at that level was so smoky and dark he could hardly see a thing. Willard was having a similar problem.

Both aviators reached Toronto safely but because of the murk neither of them landed at the agreed upon location. Willard landed at the Toronto Exhibition Grounds after covering the sixty kilometres from Hamilton in 45 minutes. Douglas landed at Toronto Island after a flight of 32 minutes. Douglas had won his bets.

Douglas was the first Canadian to receive a

pilot's licence. Most barnstormers did not bother with such formalities. They simply climbed into their planes and flew. But it was not hard to get a licence. All you had to do was take off, fly around a circle, land in one piece and demonstrate some basic knowledge of how the engine worked.

Douglas had licence number 18, dated October 5, 1910. The Aero Club of America issued the licence under the authority of the Fédération Aéronautique Internationale. The F.A.I., located in Paris, was the international organisation responsible for all flying records. No record was official unless recognized by the F. A. I.

Douglas' interests went far beyond barnstorming. Just two weeks after getting his pilot's licence, in a biplane designed by Glen Curtiss, he set a world speed record of 80 kilometres per hour at the Belmont Park International Aviation Meet in New York.

Douglas still found time for experimentation. He flew the world's first flying boat in Long Island Sound and pioneered the puller type of airplane engine. A puller was a propeller and engine mounted in the front of the aircraft, which pulled it through the air. Up until then all airplanes were of the pusher variety, that is, they were pushed through the air by a propeller and engine at the rear of the plane. In a crash, a pusher type of engine could be very dangerous. It could break loose from its mount and crush the pilot.

On August 27, 1910, Douglas sent the very first wireless, or radio, message ever transmitted from an airplane. In Palm Beach, Florida, in March of 1911, Douglas and Percy G. B. Moriss, a wireless engineer, participated in another radio experiment. This time the plan was to transmit and receive.

A wireless transmitter was set up and a lightweight receiver fitted into Douglas' airplane. Everything seemed to run smoothly except for one problem. The roar of the engine was so loud Douglas could not hear a thing over the wireless.

The solution was as simple as it was ludicrous. Percy would accompany Douglas, as a passenger, and operate the wireless. Percy put on his earphones while Douglas wrapped the man's head with wet towels, fixing them in place with wads of tape. Poor Percy looked like he was in a plaster cast. Ridiculous or not, it worked. Clear radio contact was made with the station in Palm Beach, as well as with one in Key West and with a passing steamer.

Chapter 7

Triumph and Treachery
In Cuba

With the onslaught of winter, Douglas' barnstorming show headed south. In Florida, during the winter of 1911, he decided to fly to Cuba. Up until that time no one had ever flown an airplane in Cuba. The Cuban government offered a prize of $10,000 to the first person to fly from Key West, Florida, to the capital city of Havana. Upon his acceptance of the challenge, the *Havana Post* agreed to put up an additional $5,000 and the city of Havana $3,000 more.

If successful, Douglas would break three records at once. He would make the longest flight over sea, spend the longest time airborne in powered flight, and become the first person to fly out of sight of land. The distance involved was 140 kilometres.

Douglas approached the United States Navy for help. Unlike the Canadian authorities, the Americans were keen to see what Douglas's aircraft could do. They were so eager to help that they placed the entire eastern division of their destroyer fleet at Douglas' disposal. Six ships were detailed to patrol the route and render Douglas all possible assistance.

The *Pauling* was stationed just off Havana. Stretching in a line, at roughly equal intervals, were the *Terry*, the *Drayton*, the *Roe*, the *Arthusea* and the *Forward*.

Prior to the flight the navy transported Douglas to Havana so he could choose a suitable landing field. Douglas took a second aircraft along with him so that no matter what happened during the flight he would still be able to put on an aerial show.

Douglas was a daredevil but he was not foolhardy. A cautious man who left nothing to chance, he planned to mark the course between Key West and Havana with smoke from the destroyers' funnels. It was found that the smoke could be seen for more than 20 kilometres. Rescue procedures were also discussed. A platform was built on the deck of the *Pauling*. In the event that his aircraft had to ditch at sea and was not damaged, Douglas intended to launch himself, in his aircraft, from the deck of the ship. He would never be far from rescue but his aircraft, like all other aircraft of the day, was designed for land use only. To be doubly safe he visited a Key West tinsmith and had boat-shaped pontoons fashioned and attached to the end of each wing.

Everything was now ready, except for one thing—the weather. The wind blew at a near gale force for seven days. Excitement was running at a fever pitch but so was the grumbling. No one in Key West or Cuba had ever seen an airplane before. They could not understand what was causing the delay. The onlookers did not appreciate the danger that Douglas was facing or how critical it was for him to have good weather. In Cuba, the crowds began to doubt that the young "American" was coming at all.

Around midnight on the seventh day word came that the wind was finally letting up. The decision was made to take off at dawn. But moments before the flight was to begin, a message came from the *Pauling*. The wind had started up again over Cuba. The flight was called off and the grumbling increased.

On January 28, 1911, Cuban meteorologists announced that the cyclone sweeping the straits between Havana and Key West would soon end but would be followed by a second one. In between the two storms, there would be a space of 24 hours where the sky would be calm when an attempt could be made. At 2 a.m. on January 30, the destroyers sailed to their stations. By dawn, the sea was quiet, the wind had ceased to blow and everything looked good.

Douglas was preparing his airplane in a small field, the size of a baseball diamond, in Key West. At 7:02 a.m. Douglas, ever careful, took off on what was intended to be a test flight. On the ground there was instant pandemonium. A special detachment of 30 police officers was unable to control the crowds. Nearly the entire population of Key West was pressing forward to witness Douglas' takeoff. He made two circles over the cheering crowd and headed toward Cuba. He had no other choice. People had swarmed all over the field making a landing impossible in Key West. In Havana, a cannon from the heights of sixteenth-century Morro Castle boomed out a signal that the flight was on. Thousands of Cubans gathered at the waterfront.

Douglas flew over the water at an altitude of

nearly 1,000 meters. The weather was ideal. The sun glinting off the waves was dazzling and smoke from the destroyers' funnels appeared as tiny black smudges on a canvas of intense blue. As he passed each of the destroyers he could see the sailors waving and cheering.

The flight passed without incident until Douglas was within sight of Havana. The only sound was the steady drone of the engine. Suddenly, there was an explosion only centimetres behind him. The engine coughed and began to leak oil. Desperately, he tried to coax the engine back to health, but to no avail. He was losing altitude rapidly. At 250 meters the engine stopped altogether. A connecting rod had broken through the wall of one of the cylinders and was rapidly tearing the engine apart. Douglas could do nothing but glide downward and make a landing in the sea.

The captain of the *Pauling* had been notified that Douglas had passed over the *Terry* and was in difficulty. All eyes searched the heavens. A seaman shouted, "There he is!" A spontaneous cry went up from the crew but it died on their lips.

"My God! He's falling!"

The *Pauling* headed toward Douglas, steaming at the top speed of 20 knots. The *Terry* approached from the other direction. Both vessels reached the plane at about the same time. The landing, with the aid of his homemade pontoons, was so smooth that Douglas did not even get his feet wet.

In Key West, crowds had gathered around the wireless station waiting for the news. There were groans when the word came through of Douglas' forced landing, but cheers when it was announced that both pilot and aircraft were in good shape. He had landed only two kilometres from Havana harbour. The *Pauling* picked him up in just four and one-half minutes.

"That was tough luck!" was Douglas' only comment, "Why, I could see Havana!" [1]

The airplane was not seriously damaged by the landing but was destroyed when hoisted aboard the *Terry*. The sailors wanted to get the job done quickly because three tiger sharks had been seen swimming around the plane.

As he sailed aboard the *Pauling* into Havana harbour, Douglas was surprised to discover that the Cubans considered him to be a hero. President Gomez came out to meet him and welcome him to Cuba. The President sailed aboard the *Hatuey*, flagship of the Cuban navy.

The moment he stepped on shore Douglas made his way through crowds of well-wishers to the flying field he had picked out for himself on the outskirts of the city. Climbing into his second aircraft, he put on the first barnstorming show the people of Cuba had ever seen. President Gomez was so impressed by the demonstration of "battleship bombing" that he immediately announced the formation of a school of military aviation.

Douglas was invited to be guest of honour at a state banquet. There the government of Cuba would present him with a cheque for $10,000. The *Havana Post* and the city of Havana promised to present him with their cheques as well. In all, Douglas was to receive $18,000.

The cheques from the newspaper and the city never arrived. The state dinner did take place, however. It was held amid the opulence of an opera house. President Gomez made a magnificent speech in Spanish; there were bands, crowds, and distinguished people from every part of Cuba and diplomats from all over the world. More than seven thousand invited guests gave Douglas a standing ovation. At the climax of the evening, Douglas was presented with an elaborate envelope covered in ribbons, red and green seals, and embossed with the insignia of the President of the Republic of Cuba. It contained his $10,000 cheque. Douglas was then prevailed upon to make a speech, with the Vice-President of Cuba acting as translator.

When Douglas returned to his hotel suite he opened the envelope. It contained nothing but pieces of torn newspaper; he never received his $10,000.

For a month, Douglas remained in Cuba, travelling over the island putting on air shows. Everywhere fans mobbed him. At one stop he met a wealthy cigar manufacturer who paid him $1,000 for a single flight, as well as giving him a stack of cigars one metre high.

When his stay in Cuba came to an end Douglas, who had had enough heroics for a while, decided to return to Key West by boat. He was attending a farewell party at a private seaside club when he was startled to see his boat pulling away without him. Borrowing his host's speedboat, Douglas tossed his luggage in the boat then chased the departing vessel. Unfortunately, the captain of the ship was not about to stop for any late arrivals. Near the stern were some open portholes where the ship took on coal. Douglas manoeuvred the speedboat in close and heaved his suitcases through the openings. Manoeuvring closer still, he swung himself through a porthole and landed in a heap of coal. At the time, he was dressed in a white tropical suit. When Douglas McCurdy, the hero of Cuba, returned to Key West, he was covered from head to toe in coal dust and treated like a common stowaway. Regular flights to Havana were not to be made until seventeen years later when Charles Lindbergh started an air mail service.

Chapter 8

McCurdy And

World War 1

During the remaining years before the outbreak of World War I, in 1914, Douglas continued to campaign for the establishment of a military flying corps in Canada. He made frequent trips to Ottawa, held meetings with cabinet ministers and gave speeches, calling for the formation of a squadron of twelve airplanes for the militia. Douglas was unable to make any progress. Colonel Hughes of the militia remarked that aviation had no value in war and that he did not propose to spend the government's money on such a ridiculous scheme.

In the spring of 1915, with the war in Europe raging, the Curtiss Aeroplane and Motor Company came into being. Glenn Curtiss was president of the American branch of the company and Douglas headed the Canadian branch. The purpose of the company was to manufacture the *Curtiss JN-4* or *Jenny*. The Jenny became the standard training aircraft of Canada, Britain and the United States. Altogether, Douglas' factory in Toronto produced 600 hundred machines during the war. That was nearly one-quarter of

Canada's aircraft production. Douglas also turned out the first twin engine airplane in the world, a bomber produced for the Royal Navy.

When war was declared Canada, as part of the British Empire, was involved automatically. The United States remained officially neutral until 1917, although its sympathies were with Britain and Canada. As part of her neutrality, the United States refused to export weapons of war to either side. The question was asked: what is an airplane? Was it a weapon of war? Surely, an airplane without ailerons could not be considered a weapon of war. To get around the U.S. neutrality policy, Glenn Curtiss turned out hundreds of aircraft at a plant in Buffalo, New York, then shipped them to Britain through Canada. Douglas' factory in Toronto obligingly supplied the missing ailerons.

In February, 1915, the British War Office asked the Canadian authorities for the right to recruit Canadians for the Royal Naval Air Service and the Royal Flying Corps. The Canadian government duly considered the request. Grudgingly, permission was given. An order that had made it illegal to fly an airplane within 32 kilometres of a Canadian city was set aside.

The British could recruit in Canada but there was still no flying school. To Douglas, it was obvious that he would have to act on his own. The Curtiss Flying School was founded on April 30, 1915, with Douglas as director. A seaplane base for the Royal Naval Air Service was established at Hanlan's Point on Toronto Island. An airstrip for the Royal Flying Corps was built at nearby Long Branch.

The government in Ottawa insisted that the schools be operated on a commercial basis. The students actually had to pay $400 out of their own pockets to cover the cost of instruction. This must have been one of the few times that a man had to pay for the privilege of fighting for his country. If the student completed the course satisfactorily the British would reimburse him some of the cost, give him a uniform allowance and a pre-paid second class ticket to England where he could enlist in the British services.

The students at Douglas' school started their day at 5:00 a.m. when the winds were calmest. Each student waited his turn to receive ten minutes of flight instruction at a time. In all, Douglas' students were supposed to receive 400 minutes of instruction, but this often proved impossible. In order to be acceptable for one of the British services, pilots had to be able to fly five kilometres, reach an altitude of 100 metres and glide to a safe landing with his engine switched off. It took between three and six weeks for Douglas' students to reach this level. The instruction was rough and ready but the British were very pleased with the qualities of the graduates.

Douglas' plea for the formation of a Canadian Flying Corps still received little response. It would not be until 1922 that the Canadian Air Force was finally established, a force that he had been calling for since 1909. In 1924 it became the Royal Canadian Air Force.

Up until the spring of 1917, when the two British services were merged into the Royal Air Force, more than 600 pilots were trained at Douglas' school. Among them were W. A. Curtis, Robert Leckie and Raymond Collishaw, all of whom became aces in the sky over France and later air marshals in the R.C.A.F. Another McCurdy student was Henry Arnold who became a general in the United States Army Air Force.

His job done, Douglas turned his school over to the Royal Air Force and devoted his full attention to manufacturing aircraft.

It was about this time that Douglas had to give up active flying. His vision had begun to fail and he was alarmed to discover that he could no longer make the accurate judgements required for safe take off and landing.

Throughout the 1920s and the 1930s,

Douglas acted as president of several companies that designed and manufactured commercial aircraft. It was no exaggeration to say he was the father of the aircraft industry in Canada, as much as he was of the Royal Canadian Air Force.

Chapter 9

Silver Dart Flies Again

In 1929 Curtiss Aeroplane and Motor Limited merged with another firm to become the Curtiss-Reid Aircraft Company. The new company had a factory near Montreal; Douglas served as president. Under his direction the company produced a fast manoeuvrable trainer called the *Rambler* and a prototype mail plane, the *Courier*.

Douglas was now recognized worldwide for

his aviation work. He was considered to be one of the world's greatest aircraft authorities. In 1932, when Japan invaded the Chinese province of Manchuria, it was to Douglas that the Chinese turned for assistance. The plan eventually came to naught but for a time he proposed to organize and train a corps of Canadian pilots to fight on China's behalf.

At about the same time he made a tour of Western Europe to study the problem of vibration and metal fatigue. Everywhere his reputation preceded him and he received red-carpet treatment. This was especially the case in Germany.

During the 1930s Germany had become the world leader in aviation research. Douglas was keen to tour the huge aircraft works at Bremen and Augsberg, as well as the Zeppelin plant on the shores of Lake Constance. The Germans were only too pleased to receive the Canadian visitor they had heard so much about.

Despite his many accomplishments, Douglas was a modest man and was astonished by the preparations that had been made for him. Everywhere he wished to go a chauffeured limousine or a private railcar whisked him about. In Bremen, his hotel suite came complete with a grand piano and when he visited a nightclub, the band played "The Maple Leaf Forever" as he walked in. Later, at a dinner in England, Douglas was introduced to the greatest German aircraft designer, Willy Messerschmitt. When World War II broke out in 1939, Canadians were to face deadly fighter planes designed by that same Willy Messerschmitt.

Douglas spent World War II with the Department of Munitions and Supplies as both the Assistant Director General of Aircraft Production and Director of Purchasing. Though confined to a desk, his role was invaluable. Without his tireless efforts the Royal Canadian Air Force and the air forces of our allies could not have been supplied with the weapons they needed to defeat the Nazi threat.

In tribute to his outstanding war service, Douglas was created a member of the Order of the British Empire.

In 1947, he was suprised to discover that he had been appointed to the post of Lieutenant-Governor of Nova Scotia. Upon receipt of this news, his only comment was that he would promise to fulfill his duties as well as "a country boy from Cape Breton could." [1] McCurdy adopted an open and informal style. For the next five years, until his retirement from public life, this simple country boy was the official head of the Nova Scotia Government and representative of the Crown. He opened the provincial legislature and met the great from all over Canada and the world.

After his retirement the honours continued. Undoubtedly his greatest honour occurred on February 23, 1959—the golden anniversary of his flight in 1909. On that day a re-enactment of the flight of the Silver Dart was televised for Canadians from coast to coast. Three R.C.A.F. airmen had constructed an exact replica of Douglas's airplane, the Silver Dart II, on their own time.

Just as it had been a half century before, a

strong wind swept across the ice covered surface of Bras d'Or Lake. Following a thundering flypast by the modern jet aircraft of the R.C.A.F., the *Silver Dart II*, with Wing Commander Paul Hartman at the controls, taxied across the ice and became airborne. With a twinkle in his eye, Douglas said that he might just take her up himself.

Douglas was awarded the Trans-Canada McKee Trophy in recognition of 50 years of outstanding service to Canadian aviation and was made an honorary wing commander of the R.C.A.F. His achievements were further commemorated when the post office issued a stamp depicting the *Silver Dart* in flight.

Just two years later, on June 25, 1961, John Alexander Douglas McCurdy died in Montreal at the age of 74. At the time of his death he was the oldest licensed pilot in the world. The McCurdy Award, the most prestigious honour given by the Canadian Aeronautics and Space Institute, had been named in his honour. In 1973, the name of J. A. D. McCurdy was inscribed in Canada's Aviation Hall of Fame.

Endnotes

Chapter 1
1. J.A.D. McCurdy, "The Early Days of Aviation," *Dalhousie Review*, (July 1948), p. 109.
2. H. Gordon Green, *The Silver Dart*, (Fredericton, Brunswick Press, 1959), p. 8.

Chapter 2
1. Alice Sutherland, *Canada's Aviation Pioneers*, (Toronto, McGraw-Hill Ryerson, 1978), p. 254.
2. Norman Chamberlin, "They Flew in 1909," *Canadian Aviation*, (January 1945), p. 44.

Chapter 3
1. J. A. D. McCurdy, "The Early Days of Aviation," *Dalhousie Review*, (July 1948), p. 111.
2. H. Gordon Green, *The Silver Dart*, (Fredericton, Brunswick Press, 1959), pp. 48 - 49.

Chapter 5
1. H. Gordon Green, *The Silver Dart*, (Fredericton, Brunswick Press, 1959), p. 98.
2. Norman Chamberlin, "They Flew in 1909," (*Canadian Aviation*, (January 1945), p. 47.

Chapter 6
1. *Hamilton Herald*, (July 29, 1911), p. 16.
2. *Ibid.*, (July 29, 1911), p. 16.
3. *Ibid.*, (August 3, 1911), p. 17.

Chapter 7

1. H. Gordon Green, *The Silver Dart,* (Fredericton, Brunswick Press, 1959), pp. 125 - 126.

Chapter 9

1. H. Gordon Green, *The Silver Dart,* (Fredericton, Brunswick Press, 1959), p. 159.

Bibliography

The Canadian Encyclopedia, Second Edition, Edmonton: Hurtig, 1988. "Baldwin, Frederick Walker," "Bell, Alexander Graham," "McCurdy, John Alexander Douglas," "Silver Dart."

Chamberlin, Norman. "They Flew in 1909." *Canadian Aviation* (January 1945), pp. 44-47.

Colombo, John Robert, *Colombo's Canadian References*, Toronto: Oxford University Press, 1976. "Aerial Experiment Association," "Bell, Alexander Graham," "Cygnet 1," "Hydrodrome-4," "June Bug," "Red Wing," "Silver Dart," "White Wing."

Ellis, Frank H. *Canada's Flying Heritage*. Toronto: University of Toronto Press, 1962.

Glenn H. Curtiss Museum. *The Flight of the June Bug,* Hammondsport, N. Y., Glenn H. Curtiss Museum, 1976.

Green, H. Gordon. "The Flight at Baddeck." *Atlantic Advocate* (October 1958), pp. 20-29.

Green, H. Gordon. *The Silver Dart*. Fredericton, N. B.: Brunswick Press, 1959.

Hamilton Herald, July 22, July 28, July 29, August 3 1911.

Harding, Les. "McCurdy's Cuban Adventure." Atlantic Advocate (February 1982), pp. 26 - 28.

McCurdy, J.A.D. "Canada's First Powered Flight." *Canadian Aviation* (January 1959), pp. 24-27.

McCurdy, J.A.D. "First Commonwealth Flight," *Canadian Aviation* (June 1953), pp. 82, 122-123, 142-149.

McCurdy, J.A.D. "The Early Days of Aviation," *Dalhousie Review* (July 1948), pp. 109-116.

Sutherland, Alice Gibson. *Canada's Aviation Pioneers.* Toronto, McGraw-Hill Ryerson, 1978.

Webb, Michael. *Alexander Graham Bell, Inventor of the Telephone.* Mississauga, Ont.: Copp Clark Pitman, 1991.

GLOSSARY

Aeronautical: the science or practice of motion or travel in the air

Aerodynamics: the branch of mechanics that deals with the motion of air and other gases

Aileron: a moveable surface near the end of a wing which effects the ability of an airplane to turn

Amputate: to cut off by surgical operation

Barnstorming: tricky and dangerous maneouvers done at an airshow

Bewhiskered: wearing whiskers or a beard

Biplane: type of airplane with two main sets of wings, having one above the other

Commemoration: a service or part of a service in memory of a person or event

Confederation: a union or alliance of states, etc.

Cygnet: a name which means "little swan"

Dumbfounded: confused or puzzled

Elaborate: planned with great care

Eminent: stand out above others

Epic proportions: large size

Feline: cat

Fulcrum: a part that serves as a support or hinge

Galvanize: to coat with zinc as a protection against rust

Gizmo: gadget or device

Grudgingly: unwilling or reluctant

Hamlet: a village

Impish: fun loving yet mischievous

Inscribe: write or carve words on stone, metal, paper, etc.

Ludicrous: absurd or ridiculous; laughable

Maneuver: a planned and controlled movement or series of moves

Metal fatigue: ability of a metal to handle stress

Meteorology: the study of the process and phenomena of the atmosphere, especially as a means of forecasting weather

Neutrality: refusing to take part in a war

Newfangled: new style or kind

Pandemonium: uproar; utter confusion

Patriotism: love for one's country

Pneumatic: moved or worked by air pressure

Pontoons: portable floating device

Prestigious: honored

Proposition: something offered for acceptance

Scoff: to show disrespect or lack of concern

Stable: firmly fixed or established, not easily adjusted, destroyed or altered

Tetrahedron: a triangle shape with four sides

Throttle: a valve for regulating the supply of fluid to an engine

Tinsmith: a person who makes or repairs things of sheet metal

Trainer: a machine used in training

Undercarriage: the landing gear of an airplane

Unfathomable: impossible to understand